Steam Trails

The Withered Arm

Michael Clemens

Ian Allan
PUBLISHING

INTRODUCTION

I have just finished reading again the 1965 book by E. S. Cox, *Locomotive Panorama*, Volume 1. In his opening sentence, Cox asks 'When will the well run dry?' in relation to books about railway history. Forty-two years on and still as many new books as ever are being published. What distinguishes this book compared to others 'from the well' are the photographs; while little of the written detail will probably be new, most of the photographs have never been published before.

The phrase 'The Withered Arm', relating to the Southern Railway lines of Devon and north Cornwall, seems to have come about due to SR management concentrating their efforts on the electrification of lines around London. In the inter-war period this was not just the suburban lines, but also longer-distance 'inter-city'-type routes, such as London–Brighton and London–Portsmouth. There was not much money left over to spend on lines miles away in the west, and things had to soldier on there as best as possible — they were left to wither away, although of course with such a generalisation the reality is perhaps not quite so black and white.

I have always visualised the 'Withered Arm' as an outstretched arm and hand; the long and rather isolated main line from Salisbury to Exeter is the arm, with all the connecting secondary routes and branches in the far west being the outspread fingers. There certainly seemed to be a lot of old equipment being used there, and it was not just the locomotives — much of the coaching stock for the local services was made up from demoted main-line stock.

But it is the old locomotives that are most remembered: the Beattie '0298'-class 2-4-0 well tanks (the oldest design then still running on British Railways), introduced in the 1870s, and the Adams '0415' 4-4-2 radial tanks, dating from the 1880s; while the 1890s were particularly well represented with 'M7s', 'O2s' and 'T9s'. In many ways the workhorses on the 'Withered Arm' were the 'N'-class 2-6-0s. Though dating from 1917, they were a particularly modern and successful design, quite revolutionary when the first arrived for trials on the Ilfracombe line in 1924; they stayed for 40 years. Bulleid's heavy 4-6-2s, the 'Merchant Navy' class, first saw light in the middle of World War 2, but weight restrictions kept them east of Exeter. The Bulleid light 4-6-2s appeared in 1945, their leading bogie allowing them to cope easily with all the curves on the various fingers of the 'Withered Arm', and their trailing truck allowing a large, wide firebox that gave unprecedented power, albeit with high coal consumption and high maintenance costs.

The 1950s saw the arrival of the lightweight go-anywhere Ivatt 2-6-2Ts and the British Railways 'Standards'. While the enthusiast might have preferred to see a Victorian 'T9' on his train, I think the labour-saving devices such as self-cleaning smokeboxes, rocking firegrates and hopper ashpans with bottom doors that were incorporated into the 1950s arrivals would have made them much more popular with the crews, maintenance staff and probably also the accountants. Although this is largely a steam book, it does include some of the diesel

Previous page: Pannier tank No 4666 stands at Bodmin North ready for departure to Wadebridge in the summer of 1962. The two coaches make up set number 199, one of a batch of nine sets assembled from 1936-built main-line stock that was demoted in 1960/61 for work in Devon and Cornwall. At the beginning of the 1964 Summer timetable the through trains to Wadebridge ceased, replaced by a railbus service to a newly constructed halt at Boscarne Junction, an exchange platform where connection was made with Bodmin Road–Wadebridge–Padstow trains. Complete closure at Bodmin North came in 1967.

First published 2007

ISBN (10) 0 7110 3221 1
ISBN (13) 978 0 7110 3221 7

Published by Ian Allan Publishing
an imprint of Ian Allan Publishing Ltd, Hersham, Surrey, KT12 4RG

Printed in England by Ian Allan Publishing Ltd, Hersham, Surrey, KT12 4RG

Code: 0709/B

Visit the Ian Allan Publishing website at www.ianallanpublishing.com

replacements, notably diesel multiple-units (DMUs) and North British Type 2 diesel-hydraulics ('D63xx').

The 'North Cornwall Express' ran for the first time during the summer of 1900 on the then newly built lines to Bude (1898) and Padstow (1899); another named train serving the area was the 'North Devon and Ilfracombe Express', which included dining facilities right through to Torrington. The 'Atlantic Coast Express' ('ACE'), which served stations all over the 'Withered Arm', first ran in 1926. The name was suggested by Guard F. Rowland in a staff magazine competition, for which he won a prize of 3 guineas (sadly he was the only person ever killed on the Halwill–Torrington line, following an accident at Marland in 1932). By 1927 the 'ACE' was one of the two most multi-portioned trains in the country. Starting from London Waterloo, it carried separate coaches that were progressively detached as the train headed westwards, providing both direct and indirect connections to most of the routes on the accompanying old Southern Railway map dating from around 1930.

Such was the demand that on Saturdays in the summer of 1938 the 'ACE' ran as four separate trains to distant Devon and Cornwall: 10.35am to Ilfracombe and Torrington, 10.38am to Padstow, 10.40am to Bude and 11.00am to Plymouth (Padstow and Bude). After the cutbacks of World War 2 the 1950s were boom years for the 'ACE'. However, by the end of the 1950s expanding car ownership saw a change to long-distance motoring. It was then that we started to see headlines in the papers about queues at Honiton and Okehampton; the Exeter Bypass features in my 1964 *Guinness Book of Records* with the longest traffic jam in Britain, at 30 miles, on 18 July 1964. However, even as late as 1961 there were still four separate up 'ACEs' on summer Saturdays, with the 11.00am from Padstow even running all the way to Waterloo (arrival 5.24pm) with a restaurant car.

Many of the lines we will visit belonged to the London & South Western Railway until the 1923 Grouping. Clearly the LSWR had ambitions from a very early date to expand into Devon and Cornwall. The Cornwall & Devon Central Railway, which had the active backing of the LSWR, was thrown out by the House of Lords in 1846 for not complying with Standing Orders. Following this the LSWR stepped in and took over (without Parliamentary permission) the responsibilities of the Bodmin & Wadebridge Railway, which had opened in 1834; at the time of the purchase the nearest point on the rest of the LSWR system

was Dorchester, 120 miles to the east. Gradually the LSWR expanded westwards, finally arriving at Wadebridge via the North Cornwall line in 1895, and Padstow in 1899; extensions to Newquay and Truro never materialised.

The period from the late 1950s and through the 1960s was a time of great change for the entire British Railways system, with both the elimination of steam and the closure of so many branch and secondary routes. All through this era my father was recording the changing scene, not just in the area covered by this book but all the way from Penzance to Inverness. By far the majority of the photographs were taken either by my late father or myself; most are from the years 1958-67. As we lived in Worcestershire, our photographs have come from three main sources: family holidays at Bude and Polzeath between 1961 and 1966; day trips that my father would undertake, often with his pals and me (as long as it was not during term-time); and enthusiasts' special trains on which we travelled.

In the late 1930s, as a teenager, my dad, C. N. 'Jim' Clemens (1922-87), was both an enthusiastic cyclist and a keen supporter of Exeter City Football Club. Starting at about 3.00am on Saturday mornings, my father and a friend would bicycle the approximately 125 miles from Pershore, Worcestershire, down the A38 to the football ground at St James Park, Exeter — they must have been keen Exeter supporters!

Trains to the west started at Waterloo, the last of the London termini to have regular steam working, and ran via the junction station of Basingstoke, which saw not only the usual British Railways (Southern Region) steam but also examples from 'foreign' parts. Continuing westwards, Salisbury was the main intermediate station between London and Exeter; it was rare for trains not to stop here, as generally water supplies needed to be topped up. It is easy to forget after so many years just how much interchange of traffic there used to be at Templecombe, junction for the Somerset & Dorset line. The important station at Yeovil Junction was some distance away from the town, connected by a shuttle service.

Our photographic coverage begins with the first of the East Devon branches, from Axminster to Lyme Regis, still being worked by Victorian tank engines dating from the 1880s. After looking at Sidmouth Junction, Tipton St Johns and Exmouth, we arrive at Exeter. There was plenty of activity to be seen at the old LSWR station here, rebuilt during

Above: The Way West: 'Merchant Navy' No 35028 *Clan Line* awaits departure from London Waterloo on 5 March 1964. By 1927 the 'Atlantic Coast Express' was one of the two most multi-portioned trains in the country, the other being the 'Cornish Riviera Express'. The rear coach was shed at Salisbury and was worked forward by the succeeding slow train, eventually terminating at Seaton. Two came off at Sidmouth Junction, one for Sidmouth, one for Exmouth. The restaurant cars came off at Exeter and the train split in two: the Ilfracombe section, which dropped off a Torrington portion at Barnstaple Junction, and the Padstow section, which dropped off a portion for Plymouth at Okehampton and a portion for Bude at Halwill. Nine separate portions with 11 locomotives sharing in their haulage!

Above: It's 9.58am on Sunday 12 September 1965 and the Southern Counties Touring Society (SCTS) 'Exeter Flyer' is arriving at Basingstoke. With the Southern Region having no water troughs, the non-stop run to Exeter from here was notable for the distance run without liquid refreshment — 124 miles. The tour was no slowcoach either: between Wilton South and Exmouth Junction (84½ miles) the average speed was over 70mph. No 35022 *Holland-America Line* was a member of the SR's most powerful class, the 'Merchant Navy' 4-6-2s. It is coupled to one of the large-water-capacity tenders, holding 6,000 gallons and five tons of coal.

Left: Here at Battledown flyover, west of Basingstoke, the London–Bournemouth and London–Exeter routes diverge, although the actual physical junction is at Worting. Having just passed over the Exeter lines, 'Merchant Navy' No 35008 *Orient Line* heads for Waterloo with a train from Bournemouth on 22 June 1967.

Above: As the SR had no water troughs, its long-distance services had to stop and fill up with water. No 35028 *Clan Line* has just arrived at Salisbury after a fast run down from Waterloo on 5 March 1964, 83¾ miles scheduled in 80 minutes. In addition to topping up the water, coal was brought forward in the tender for the onward journey to Exeter, and all this in 4 minutes. Soon after Nationalisation water troughs were considered for this route and the Bournemouth line, with proposed installations at Farnborough, Milborne Port and Millbrook. However, on reflection it was felt that the need for non-stop running did not justify the costs, and nothing came of the proposals.

Above right: A shabby No 34002 *Salisbury* has just arrived at Yeovil Junction on 27 March 1963 with the westbound through service from Brighton to Plymouth. This important restaurant-car train had through carriages from Portsmouth and was used by Royal Navy personnel. Yeovil Junction had two island platforms with four tracks between them, the centre pair being through tracks for non-stopping services. It was felt that there was no need for two main lines to London from Exeter, and this LSWR route was downgraded during 1967 in favour of the GWR line via Taunton; surprisingly, the turntable (partly visible in front of No 34002) survived and is still used today by visiting preserved steam.

Right: The Salisbury–Exeter main line was the last in the country to retain steam haulage on all the expresses, the final steam 'Atlantic Coast Express' running on 5 September 1964. The route was something of a switchback but with little in the way of speed restrictions (at Wilton, and in the up direction only at Seaton Junction). In the steam era it was reckoned to have the highest average speeds in the world considering the gradients involved. This lovely shot of an eastbound cattle train near Tisbury together with a flooded River Sem dates from the spring of 1964.

1933 and renamed from Queen Street to Central by the Southern Railway, with much splitting and reforming of trains. To a young lad in early 1964 the former GWR station at Exeter St Davids seemed to present such a contrast — the former LSWR routes with steam and the GWR routes with diesel.

After Exeter, specifically at Cowley Bridge Junction, we move on to the 'Withered Arm' proper. On the way round the north of Dartmoor to Plymouth we visit Okehampton and the famous Meldon viaduct. A somewhat later railway opening, in 1908, was the Plymouth, Devonport & South Western Junction line from Bere Alston through Gunnislake to Callington; this is seen in both 1961 and 1965.

The line from Coleford Junction through Eggesford and Umberleigh to Barnstaple (Junction) is still open today; Barnstaple shed once played host to both the old 'M7' and the new Ivatt Class 2 tank engines, together with GWR Moguls from Taunton. After crossing the River Taw we arrive at Barnstaple Town before visiting Ilfracombe.

Following the River Torridge the railway arrives at Torrington, where there was an end-on junction with one of the last examples of new railway construction in this country for many decades. The impressive-sounding North Devon & Cornwall Junction Light Railway, which opened as late as 1925, is covered in some detail, down to one of the most famous rural railway junctions in the UK — Halwill.

As we holidayed at Bude a number of times, there is naturally excellent coverage here, including the line from Halwill, the harbour branch, the Bude Canal itself, and the Sand Tramway. To reach Padstow we journey down the North Cornwall Railway, stopping off at Launceston, Camelford and Wadebridge. Wadebridge was, of course, famous for another of the Victorian survivals, the Beattie well tanks; in addition to station pilot duties they are seen along the Wenford Bridge branch. We also visit Bodmin North in 1962, which had opened in 1834 when it was just plain Bodmin.

In the years following Nationalisation in 1948, despite some changing of regional boundaries, the 'Withered Arm' remained pretty much intact and steam operated until 1962. The competing company in the South West was the Great Western Railway, and its successor, the Western Region of British Railways. By 1962 the WR had already shut down various branches in the area and was well on the way to the elimination of steam. At midnight on 31 December 1962, during a blizzard that had begun four days before, the WR gained control of the SR lines west of Wilton, near Salisbury. It did not take long for the process of what has been called 'Westernisation' to take place. The duplicate routes from Exeter to London were seen as a waste of resources, and the WR announced that the Paddington route was to be the main line. The old SR route was demoted to a semi-fast diesel service and eventually singled for much of the distance west of Salisbury. It seemed that in no time at all steam was being replaced all over the 'Withered Arm' by diesel multiple-units and the unreliable 'D63xx' diesel-hydraulics. Freight services started to be withdrawn, as this did not involve the regulatory processes needed to close down a passenger service. I recall talking to a hotel owner in Bude who was convinced that the railway would carry on; she was wrong. Torrington was served by 24 through coaches from Waterloo on summer Saturdays in 1955, but none at all by the end of 1963. The signalbox at Halwill was reckoned to be the largest on any single-line system in the country, with four separate lines converging; everything was intact in 1964, but the first line (to Torrington) had gone by 1965 and the other three by 1966. This was repeated all across the area, so that by the early 1970s the system was but a shadow of its former self.

Looking back, I'm not sure it all can be blamed on 'Westernisation'. The evidence of declining traffic was there to see, and in some ways it appears that the SR chose to ignore it. The Bude branch and the North Cornwall line still had passing loops and staff at every station, with a traffic level that did not really justify them. Perhaps if economies had been made earlier, places like Ilfracombe, Bideford, Bude, Wadebridge and Padstow would still be on the railway map, with the main line still open through Okehampton and Tavistock — but it was not to be. Hopefully this book will go some way to showing how things were during the last years on the 'Withered Arm'.

Michael Clemens
Pershore, Worcestershire
April 2007

Right: The author was only six when he travelled with his father on this Gloucestershire Railway Society tour, seen here by the down platform at Axminster on 10 May 1958. The three-car 'Cross-Country' diesel multiple-unit (DMU) looks in pristine condition, and the crew seem to be getting instructions on how to cross over to the Lyme Regis branch. Axminster had opened in 1860 and by 1870 there was double track; the down platform was extended in 1938, and this can be seen beyond the road bridge. On 11 June 1967 the WR singled the line; today the footbridge has been demolished and just the down platform is used.

2nd - DAY EXCUSION
MAY 10th 1958
GLOUCESTERSHIRE RAILWAY SOCIETY
Cheltenham Spa (St. James) P. to
LYME REGIS
and BACK
Out via Gloucester, Mangotsfield, Cole &
Templecombe
Return via Yeovil, Radstock, Filton Jct.,
Standish Jct. & Gloucester.
(W)   For conditions see over
074   074

Left: As far back as 1871 a line had been authorised from Axminster to Lyme Regis, but the powers lapsed, and it was not until 1899 that a Light Railway Order was obtained to build the 6¾-mile branch, which opened on 24 August 1903. The line departs westwards from a bay platform on the up side of Axminster station, where Adams radial 4-4-2 tank No 30583 is seen on 10 May 1958. Being a light railway it required appropriate light motive power, and, following successful trials in 1916, these locomotives were used on the branch until 1961, when the Ivatt 2-6-2Ts were permitted after some track modifications.

The Gloucestershire Railway Society DMU special of 10 May 1958 stands at the main platform face at Lyme Regis, which could accommodate six coaches. The station was 250ft above sea level. Freight traffic was accommodated in three sidings and consisted largely of coal, cement, slag and fertiliser. There was also considerable traffic for local shops, including one wagon a week for Messrs Boots from Beeston, Nottinghamshire. A single-unit diesel railcar took over services in November 1963, and freight facilities were withdrawn. Steam did return for a while in February 1965, due to a shortage of railcars, until the Halwill–Torrington service ceased. The final trains ran on 27 November 1965.

Right: The signalbox at Lyme Regis was at the end of the platform, although the tablet instrument was in the booking office, as the signalman performed clerical duties as well. Behind the signalbox is a short bay with a cattle dock. The post with the curved overhanging arm is a loading gauge, to check that wagons from the goods yard had not been filled to greater than the railway's clearances. Behind it is the single-road engine shed for the branch locomotive, which at the time of this 10 May 1958 photograph was Adams radial tank No 30583.

Left: No 30583 is running round at Lyme Regis after arrival from Axminster on 10 May 1958. This severely curved line was well known as the last haunt of these Adams radial tanks, whose flexible wheelbase could cope with the branch conditions. Introduced in 1882 for London suburban services, the class eventually totalled 71. By 1930 the only two SR members left were on this branch, but a pair was not enough for long-term needs, and a third was discovered rusting away in 1946 on the East Kent Railway, having been sold off during World War 1. This was repaired at Eastleigh Works and became No 30583 in BR days; today it is preserved and on the Bluebell Railway in East Sussex.

Back on the SR's West of England main line, we see the 'Atlantic Coast Express' pulling away from Sidmouth Junction on 5 March 1964 behind No 35028 *Clan Line*; the next stop, Exeter Central, is 12½ miles away. No 35028 slipped badly on starting, and when the author visited again, on 31 March, No 35014 had to set back before getting away. The Bulleid 'Pacifics' were prone to slipping, in fact this was a problem that afflicted all 4-6-2s in the country. Locomotive designer E. S. Cox, who lived in Sidmouth, regarded the problem as unfinished business. His suggestion (as in American practice) would have been to equalise, with compensated springing, the weight between the coupled and carrying wheels, but the extra weight and space needed were major problems.

Right: The first railway to Sidmouth was proposed in 1862, but it was not until 6 July 1874 that this 8¼-mile branch through Tipton St Johns actually opened. Until 1881 the station was called plain Tipton, and it became a junction when the line to Budleigh Salterton opened on 15 May 1897. Looking north towards Ottery St Mary and Sidmouth Junction on 5 March 1964, this single railcar has just arrived from Budleigh Salterton. Closure to passengers came on 6 March 1967, to be followed by complete closure two months later, on 8 May. Today the station building survives as a private residence together with part of one of the platforms.

Right: There is plenty to see at the south end of Tipton St Johns station on 5 March 1964. To the left is the Sidmouth branch climbing away at 1 in 45; the two-coach DMU is a through service from Sidmouth Junction, having connected with the 'Atlantic Coast Express'. The line on the right had opened as far as Budleigh Salterton in 1897, the extension on to Exmouth opening on 1 June 1903. A single railcar is approaching from Exmouth and will terminate here; clearly any passengers wanting to travel on to Sidmouth will have missed the connection shown in the timetable.

Left: According to Exmouth station clock it is 2.40pm, and the date is a misty 5 March 1964. The single railcar on the left has worked in on a service from Tipton St Johns, while the three-car unit on the right will soon be departing for Exeter Central. The large station here had opened in 1861 with the arrival of the Exeter & Exmouth Railway, the Tipton St Johns line opening throughout in 1903. The station was rebuilt by the SR in 1927, and nowadays, although just a single platform, it has an interval service along the Exe estuary to Exeter with an annual passenger usage of 611,000. The Tipton St Johns route closed in 1967.

Left: The weather is clearly a lot better in this panoramic view of Exmouth station taken on 13 October 1959, with Standard Class 3 tank No 82017 leaving on the 1.45pm to Exeter. The ten locomotives in the series 82010-19 were turned out from Swindon Works between June and September 1952 and all were initially allocated to Exmouth Junction shed. Here they replaced the elderly 'M7' 0-4-4Ts on the Exmouth services plus local trains to Honiton and Axminster. Following the transfer in of Standard Class 4 tanks in 1962, No 82017 was re-allocated to Eastleigh and then Nine Elms; withdrawal came in April 1965 and it was cut up for scrap in Morriston, South Wales.
Ian Allan Library

Two Ivatt Class 2 tank engines are on Exmouth shed in September 1962; note the two different styles of chimney. A small wooden engine shed was constructed close by New Street on opening of the line in 1861, but the shed visible here dates from when the station was rebuilt in the 1920s. The new shed was built in ferro-concrete from the Exmouth Junction Works and was surmounted by a new water tank, replacing a previous unreliable supply. The shed originally had a turntable but this was removed during the reconstruction when found to be beyond repair; total cost of the scheme was £2,200. The shed closed on 8 November 1963 and has been demolished, the site covered by a new road. *Ian Allan Library*

Exeter Queen Street was the original terminus of the Exeter extension of the London & South Western Railway and opened on 19 July 1860; it was rebuilt and renamed Central on 1 July 1933. At the east end of the station on 15 June 1963 an Exmouth service (position 1 disc codes on both locomotives) is about to depart from the up bay platform. On the left the scissors crossings on the up main side are clearly visible. The nearest locomotive is an LMS-designed Ivatt Class 2, one of the batch of 30 constructed at Crewe in the early 1950s specifically for Southern Region services. The rear locomotive is one of the BR Standard Class 4 tanks transferred to Exmouth Junction the previous summer. Out of sight there is another on the rear of the coaches.

Left: 'Battle of Britain' 4-6-2 No 34062 *17 Squadron* is heading for Salisbury, also on 15 June 1963. Growth of traffic taxed accommodation here and in 1925 this platform was extended to 1,200ft, with scissors crossovers provided to enable two up trains to be dealt with simultaneously. No 34062 has a tender full of coal and will have been serviced at Exmouth Junction shed before taking over this train from the west.

Left: On the same day 'Battle of Britain' No 34063 *229 Squadron* is leaving Exeter Central with a three-coach train, heading towards its home depot of Salisbury. The disc codes in positions 1 and 5, above and below the front number, indicate a service between Plymouth and Waterloo (or Nine Elms). Visibility of disc codes was a problem in the dark, and the Bulleid 'Pacifics' had a steam turbo-generator, which is supplying the electrically lit headcode lamps visible on No 34063; it also supplied inspection lights. Behind in the bay platform is an Exmouth service, already converted to DMU operation by this time.

Exeter Central's two main platforms (up at 1,200ft, down at 950ft) were separated by four through roads arranged in pairs, with a set of scissors crossings on the up side for amalgamating trains, adding restaurant cars etc. The date is 15 June 1963, and 'N'-class 2-6-0 No 31844 is on a short up freight, with the large goods depot behind. There was much changing of locomotives here on the through passenger trains to and from the west; goods services, however, would change engines at Exmouth Junction.

Right: Nos 80039 and 80043 are at the west end of Exeter Central on Sunday 12 September 1965, about to take the 'Exeter Flyer' tour onwards to Ilfracombe and Torrington. Exmouth Junction shed had closed some months earlier, so the two Standard Class 4 tanks were specially brought in from Templecombe, nearly 60 miles away to the east. The lines west of Exeter were unable to take the heavier express locomotives, and it was usual for arrivals from London to be replaced here. The half-mile connecting line between Central and St Davids stations was opened in 1862 and involved a falling gradient of 1 in 37.

Right: Beyond Exeter the line skirted the northern slopes of Dartmoor to reach Okehampton, where we see the 'Exmoor Ranger' tour on 27 March 1965 after arrival from Exeter. The signalbox on the up platform was in use from 12 May 1935 to 10 July 1972. Although it gives the impression of being a single-storey building, because the station was on a hillside with the ground falling away, the structure was quite tall. Above the footbridge is the top arm of the up co-acting starter signal; with arms at both the top and bottom of the post, the lower one gave good visibility when close to, but was obscured when seen from a distance, as here, so was repeated by the upper arm against the sky.

A verdant view of Meldon Viaduct showing an Exmouth Junction to Plymouth Friary freight passing over; although dated 1963, it is unlikely to be that year. This Standard Class 4 4-6-0 is fitted with both a double chimney and the smaller type BR2 tender with an inset coal bunker. The SR series with double chimneys all had larger capacity tenders that were physically much bigger; this means that it was one of the twenty initially allocated to the WR and built between 1951 and 1954 at Swindon Works, some of which were later equipped with a double chimney. Exmouth Junction did receive some of these during the period 1964/65; the three locomotives concerned were Nos 75005/08/22. *John Parsons*

Right: An August 1961 view of Meldon Viaduct from the south: to the right can be seen the single coach for the Okehampton–Meldon Quarry service used by staff and families, parked at the end of the quarry shunting neck. The gradient on the viaduct is 1 in 77, afterwards increasing to 1 in 58 on the down (left) side. The original single-line wrought iron span of 1874 suffered from subsequent movement of the cast iron supporting piers, which were set into granite blocks; when the second bridge, this time with steel girders, was built and opened in 1879 it was interlaced with the first, as is clearly visible, which cured the movement problem.

Right: This photograph of the same side of Meldon Viaduct as the one above is the most modern in the book and was taken on 18 March 1990. The viaduct is still in existence today and was, in its modern refurbished form, formally opened on 6 July 2002 by TV science presenter Adam Hart-Davis. Meldon Viaduct now forms part of the Okehampton to Lydford 'Granite Way' which itself is part of the Devon 'Coast to Coast' cycle route. The still active quarry is behind us and nearby is the Meldon Dam and Reservoir. *R. E. Ruffell*

The view south across Meldon Viaduct on Saturday 20 April 1974, during the visit of the 'Devon Rambler' railtour. The entire structure was built on a curve of 30-chain radius, and the six spans had a maximum height of 140ft above the valley of the West Okement River. Services across the viaduct finished on 6 May 1968, but in the 1970s a shunting neck was reopened over part of it, the better to serve Meldon Quarry.

The up 'Atlantic Coast Express' is passing over Meldon Viaduct behind unrebuilt 'West Country' No 34030 *Watersmeet* on 3 June 1959 as No 34064 *Fighter Command* is shunting hoppers into the quarry sidings. Visible between the two locomotives in the distance is the embankment that No 34030 has just passed over before joining the Plymouth line at Meldon Junction, involving 15 chain radius curves. In April 1962 No 34064 was fitted with a Giesl oblong ejector type of chimney in an a effort to overcome the poor steaming/lack of draught experienced after fitting spark-arresting equipment; this was the last technical alteration to the Bulleid Pacifics, although it was really too late in the day for steam to be of value. *Brian Haresnape*

Above: The Plymouth, Devonport & South Western Junction Railway opened its route from Lydford to Plymouth on 2 June 1890, leased to and operated by the London & South Western Railway. This finally gave the LSWR independent access to Plymouth from London and Exeter, instead of having to use the Great Western line from Lydford to Plymouth. This Whitsun 1965 view, looking towards Plymouth at the junction station of Bere Alston, shows a Callington-bound service in the far platform. The section north from here to Tavistock and Okehampton closed to all traffic, as far as Meldon Quarry, on 6 May 1968.

Right: The view is looking west from Bere Alston on 9 June 1965; to the left is the double-track line to Plymouth from Exeter, while to the right a Callington-bound service has just departed. The Callington branch was both steep, with frequent gradients of between 1 in 38 and 1 in 50, and serpentine, with numerous curves sharper than 10-chain radius. Although the section on to Callington closed in 1966, because of the poor road access to Plymouth from this part of Devon and Cornwall the railway survives as the 'Tamar Valley line', with a shuttle service from Gunnislake

Below: The GWR diehards must have been upset on 3 May 1964, the day of the last steam train to Penzance. A special train was run, from Exeter to Plymouth and return (via Newton Abbot); GWR heavy freight 2-8-0 No 2887 was used. However, on the GWR route from Plymouth to Penzance and back the train was hauled by an unrebuilt SR Bulleid 'West Country' Pacific. A very smartly turned out No 34002 *Salisbury* is seen at Plymouth after arriving back with the 'Cornubian' tour from Penzance; apparently the crew were impressed with its performance. Retribution for the WR taking over the SR lines west of Salisbury?

Right: This 1965 view of Gunnislake station on the Callington branch from Bere Alston was taken from a Callington–Bere Alston diesel railcar. The island platform was accessed by a short passenger subway, and it was the only station on the branch where two passenger trains could pass, the signalling being controlled by the ground frame visible on the extreme right. The 3ft 6in-gauge East Cornwall Mineral Railway built its Drakewalls Depot here in 1872, which became Gunnislake station in 1908 when the line was reconstructed to standard gauge and extended across the Tamar. In 1994 the station, by then the branch terminus, was moved slightly to the south, eliminating a low-headroom bridge over the A390.

Right: Class O2 0-4-4 tank No 30225 stands outside the shed at Callington on Friday 26 May 1961. By this time the Adams-designed 'O2s' were around 70 years old, the first in the class of 60 having been built in 1889 and the last in 1895. They were drafted in during 1929 and worked on the line up to 1961, when the Ivatt '2MT' 2-6-2 tanks took over all workings until dieselisation in 1964. Although normally used on the passenger services, the maximum number of wagons allowed for an 'O2' between Gunnislake and Callington was 12, the limit for the 2-6-2Ts being 20.

Above: The railway first arrived at Callington during 1872, in the form of the narrow-gauge East Cornwall Mineral Railway (not authorised to carry passengers) from Calstock Quay, on the River Tamar. Eventual connection to the national rail system at Bere Alston came in 1908, which was done by both new construction and conversion of the existing narrow-gauge line. Callington station was actually in Kelly Bray, about a mile from the town, and is seen here during the Whitsun half-term school holidays in 1965. One locomotive used to be stabled in the wooden engine shed, with another outside on the same road; the other track was used for locomotive coal wagons.

We now turn our attention to the Coleford Junction–Barnstaple line. On 12 September 1965 the 'Exeter Flyer' had a 10-minute stop at Eggesford passing loop on the way from Exeter to Barnstaple Junction. Originally opened as broad-gauge in 1854, the line became mixed-gauge in 1863 and standard-gauge only from 1877. Barnstaple Junction shed had closed to steam in November 1964 and Exmouth Junction in May 1965, and as this was to be the last steam working to Torrington (with No 80043) and Ilfracombe (No 80039), the locomotives were borrowed from Templecombe. So oversubscribed was the trip that it was repeated on 3 October with the same locomotives, although their destinations were reversed.

The author's first family holiday to Cornwall, at Bude, was during the Whitsun school break in 1961. The journey down from Pershore, Worcestershire (much of it on the A38), on Saturday 20 May, seemed to go on and on, but stops were made at a couple of stations. The first was Wiveliscombe, but this is Umberleigh.

The bridge in the background is the road taken that day from South Molton to Torrington, the B3227. Unrebuilt 'West Country' No 34002 *Salisbury* is making its way from Barnstaple Junction to Exeter. Umberleigh station clearly shows its broad-gauge origins, with a wider space than normal between the up and down tracks.

Left: Parked outside Barnstaple Junction shed, on the track that led to the lifting crane, is 'M7' No 30254. Also partly visible in this 28 May 1961 photograph is Ivatt Class 2 No 41294, its bunker stacked high with coal. The wooden shed had an unusual form of illumination using window frames; there were more than half a dozen of them on the opposite (west) side. The timber building appears to have been built by the LSWR *c*1863/4, when the company's standard-gauge engines started running between Exeter and Bideford. An 1874 plan shows one of the shed roads fitted out as mixed-gauge, ie capable of accepting both broad and standard-gauge locomotives.

Left: This is the south end of Barnstaple Junction shed on the same day, coded 72E at this time. Visible on the left-hand shed road is unrebuilt 'Battle of Britain' Pacific No 34081 *92 Squadron*, with an Ivatt Class 2 behind it; on the right is GWR-built 2-6-0 No 7326, which will have worked in from Taunton. The GWR used to have a separate station and shed at Barnstaple Victoria Road, but the shed there closed in January 1951. On the left is the goods shed; between it and the locomotive shed was the access to various goods sidings for local traders.

Right: At the north (back) end of Barnstaple Junction shed on Sunday 28 May 1961 was found this row of coaled-up locomotives. Visible are four Class M7 0-4-4Ts, together with one of the newcomers from the 1950s that replaced them — an Ivatt Class 2 2-6-2T (apparently No 41312, since preserved). To the left of the locomotives can be seen part of the goods yard, while to their right is the lifting crane. There was a quite large workshop department here that could cope with most repairs; its skills were rated more highly by the locomen than those of the main SR shed for Devon and Cornwall at Exmouth Junction.

Left: Oh dear! Barnstaple Junction shed's roof looks in a very poor way in this 1963 photograph. Despite appearances, however, it remained open for steam until 1964. On view is unrebuilt 'West Country' No 34020 *Seaton;* the rebuilt engines were too heavy for the route from Coleford Junction. Behind is Ivatt Class 2 No 41224, one of the locomotives transferred from the LMR during the early 1960s; in 1962 it was allocated to Wellingborough (15A). The large buildings to the right (that clearly once had rail access) housed the stores, repair shop, forge, office and mess; the small building in front was the toilet.

Seen from what was then the A39 road bridge, No 80039 is coming off the single-line section and arriving at Barnstaple Junction from Ilfracombe on 12 September 1965. While most of the Ilfracombe line was double-tracked between 1889 and 1891, the three-quarter-mile section from Barnstaple Junction across the River Taw viaduct, through Barnstaple Town station and on to Pottington signalbox was left as single line; it also had sharp reverse curves of 7¼- and 7½-chain radius. In the July 1970 *Railway Magazine*, three months before closure, it was reported that Lord Wakefield was considering buying and operating the 15-mile line, but clearly nothing came of it.

Right: Ivatt Class 2 2-6-2 tank No 41314 is heading out of Barnstaple Junction for Torrington showing the correct headcode disc, whilst visible in the station is a Bulleid Pacific showing the disc position for an Ilfracombe service; it will take the tracks curving away to the left. The first North Devon Railway train from Exeter, conveying special guests, arrived here for a ceremonial opening on 12 July 1854. From Umberleigh into Barnstaple the North Devon laid its tracks on the abandoned earthworks of the Taw Valley Railway. The fourth line to reach Barnstaple Junction was the Devon and Somerset (later GWR) line from Taunton, this gained access to the, by then, standard-gauge-only Barnstaple Junction in 1887. Today only the Exeter line survives. *J. Davenport*

Right: Train 2C87 from Ilfracombe to Exeter is crossing the River Taw between Barnstaple Town and Barnstaple Junction on 2 September 1965, hauled by North British Type 2 diesel-hydraulic D6334. The poor exterior condition was a result of mechanical cleaning systems, particularly the one at Plymouth Laira depot. There were 58 members of this class, the first six of which were to a different design of less power, and all entered service between January 1959 and November 1962. They saw extensive use on mainly secondary services throughout the south-west on both the old GWR and SR systems. Not regarded as a particularly successful class, the first to be withdrawn was in December 1967 although D6334 survived until October 1971. *R. Howells*

Left: The first locomotive to pass over the River Taw viaduct at Barnstaple did so on 16 June 1874. The viaduct underwent its official Board of Trade inspection, using two locomotives weighing about 80 tons and lasting two hours, supervised by Colonel Hutchinson on 13 July 1874. It didn't quite achieve its centenary of service, as the line on to Ilfracombe from Barnstaple Junction was closed from 5 October 1970 and the viaduct later dismantled. This undated view looking towards the north bank shows very rusty looking tracks and what appear to be fishermen on the viaduct, so presumably is after closure! *D. Doble*

Right: Barnstaple Town station on 28 May 1961, showing the Ilfracombe line on the left platform face. The right face was where the narrow-gauge (1ft 11½in) Lynton & Barnstaple Railway used to depart; this had opened in 1898, but the final services ran on 29 September 1935.

On 12 September 1965 the last but one steam locomotive to visit Ilfracombe, BR Standard Class 4 tank No 80039, is slowly crossing (maximum speed 15mph) the sharply curved 16-span viaduct over the River Taw at Barnstaple, on its way between Junction and Town stations.

Left: Regular steam working to Ilfracombe had finished by the time the 'Exmoor Ranger' tour visited on 27 March 1965. The line had been doubled throughout from Pottington signalbox at Barnstaple by 1891, although only one platform with two faces was ever provided at Ilfracombe. The now preserved Collett 0-6-0 No 3205 is preparing to tackle the climb of 1 in 36 to Mortehoe & Woolacombe, assisted at the rear by two Ivatt 2-6-2 tanks — three locomotives but only five coaches! No 3205 will then continue alone to Barnstaple before taking the ex-GWR line on to Dulverton and Taunton.

Right: 'M7' 0-4-4T No 30023 has arrived at Instow during August 1961 on a Barnstaple Junction–Torrington train. The first line in the area, the horse-drawn Taw Valley Railway, had opened from Barnstaple to Fremington Quay in 1848. In 1855 it was extended on to Instow and Bideford, and originally this section was broad-gauge. A third rail was laid in 1863, allowing both broad and standard-gauge services until April 1877, when the broad gauge was abolished. Although passenger services finished in 1965, freight carried on through Instow until 1982. Today this site has been restored by the Bideford & Instow Railway Group.

Right: The 6.38pm Barnstaple Junction–Torrington service is running along the east bank of the River Torridge between Instow and Bideford. No 41313 was transferred away from North Devon in 1963 and withdrawn from Eastleigh in June 1965. It was lucky enough to be sent to the famous Woodham's scrapyard in South Wales; many of the locomotives sent here were not cut up and they just slowly rusted away year after year. Later purchased by the Ivatt Trust and moved to Quainton (Buckinghamshire Railway Centre) in 1975, it was used as a source of spares. The Trust came to an agreement with the Isle of Wight Steam Railway to restore No 41313 to working order and the locomotive arrived there in August 2006, having spent over 40 years out of use. *J. C. Beckett*

Right: This is Torrington station on Thursday 24 August 1961 just before 4.00pm. 'M7' No 30253 is taking water, having just arrived from Barnstaple Junction with a through portion of the 'Atlantic Coast Express' from London. Adjacent to the water column is a 'fire devil'; during cold weather this was used to keep a coal fire burning, the heat of which stopped the water column from freezing up. In the background an Ivatt Class 2 is shunting the yard, while another is waiting to form the 4.0pm departure to Halwill. The timetable was well thought out, even the likes of remote Watergate Halt having excellent connections to and from London.

This lovely panoramic shot of Torrington station and yards was taken on Saturday 15 June 1963. Ivatt Class 2 tank engines abound: No 41210 is taking water after having just arrived from Barnstaple Junction, and No 41313 is in the left background, soon to come into the station with the afternoon Halwill service. Another is shunting the goods yard, and a fourth is hiding at the head of two coaches on the left beyond the station buildings, near where the engine shed used to be (closed in 1959). Enthusiasts will note three different styles of chimney: No 41210 with the original 'short and fat', the locomotive in the goods yard from the 4129x series with a 'tall and thin', and No 41313 with the final, well-proportioned version!

A car that had both style and performance in the austerity years after World War 2 was the Jowett Javelin; standing in front of No 41210 at Torrington on the same day, MTA 389 (an Exeter plate) glints in the sunshine. The station sign will have come from the concrete works at Exmouth Junction, as did masses of other concrete products, from prefabricated lengths of platform to lamp posts. Although a 'foreign' (London, Midland & Scottish Railway) design, so successful were the 30 Ivatt Class 2s (Nos 41290-41319) built specifically for the Southern Region in the 1950s that others were transferred in later, doubling the total and enabling withdrawal of the elderly 'M7s'. No 41210 shows its LMS ancestry with vacuum-type push-pull apparatus on the smokebox; the Southern used compressed air.

The 'Exeter Flyer' railtour on 12 September 1965, hauled by No 80043, was going to be the last visit by steam to Torrington. However, as mentioned earlier, the tour was so popular that it ran again on 3 October (the same weekend that regular passenger trains ceased), when No 80039 was the train locomotive. Note the tankers for the milk-loading depot at the back of the goods shed; despite it being a Sunday there is a North British Type 2 diesel-hydraulic in the yard for working this. The milk business was transferred to road in 1978. A special very last passenger train to Torrington ran on Saturday 6 November 1982 with Class 31/1 diesels Nos 31 158 and 31 174.

The North Devon & Cornwall Junction Light Railway (ND&CJLR), which opened in 1925, entered Torrington from the south after crossing the River Torridge on this 700ft-long, 40ft-high curving steel viaduct that rested on ten stone piers, seen here in 1963. This structure replaced the earlier wooden 'fan'-type viaduct of the narrow-gauge Torrington & Marland Railway, dating from 1881. The engineer for this original line was J. B. Fell, whose name is associated with very steep mountain railways around the world, including the Snaefell Mountain Railway on the Isle of Man. Fell saw the Torrington & Marland as a testbed for his ideas about economy and speed of construction for light railways.

The author has always been intrigued by the more obscure services in railway timetables. Table 48 of the Southern Region services was just such an example, and an opportunity to sample the delights of the ND&CJLR came on Tuesday 23 May 1961. The plan was that the author would be met at Watergate Halt by his father, who, having asked the traincrew to keep an eye on his son, would drive from Halwill, but, despite the slow speed of the train (77 minutes for 18¾ miles — an average of 14.6mph), nobody was there to collect him. As the single-coach train pulls away everyone appears to be looking back at nine-year-old Michael, left on his own in the middle of nowhere!

Right: The 'Exmoor Ranger' tour of 27 March 1965 made a photographic stop at Watergate Halt, set amongst the woods and rhododendrons, before continuing down the Pencleave Valley to Torrington. Nos 41206 and 41291 simmer away as enthusiasts clamber around this remote stretch of line, which had opened for passengers on 20 September 1926; the last normal service train had stopped just four weeks before this tour. The main purpose of the halt and its adjacent siding, which closed on 2 May 1960, appears to have been as a central point for the collection of pit props for use in the clay pits down the line. The name probably came from nearby Watergate Bridge — it certainly had nothing to do with President Nixon!

Right: On Thursday 24 August 1961 the author's father used this ticket to travel out from Torrington on the 4.0pm Halwill passenger service as far as Petrockstow; he then immediately caught the 4.37pm mixed train back to Torrington, persuading the guard to allow him to travel in the brake van. By the early 1960s virtually the only regular passenger traffic comprised 30-40 clay workers. The Ivatt tank has breasted Yarde Summit and is now coasting downhill to Torrington, the scenery here contrasting with the bleak uplands of the southern section of the ND&CJLR.

Three passengers are waiting at Yarde Halt, 16 miles and 5 chains from Halwill, on 23 May 1961 for the mid-morning service to Torrington. Yarde Halt provided more passenger traffic than any other intermediate station or halt on the line, and a small waiting shelter was situated at the foot of the ramp. A row of cottages built for clay workers was close by. Although the through route opened on 27 July 1925, Yarde opened a year later on 19 July 1926. It was the only intermediate station with no sidings and had a life of less than 40 years, the last passenger trains calling on 27 February 1965.

Right: The check rail in the foreground is evidence of the ND&CJLR's sharp curves, as seen from an up train hauled by Ivatt Class 2 No 41314 between Dunsbear Halt and Yarde Halt on 23 May 1961. On the completely new route south from Dunsbear few curves were less than 20 chains radius and no gradients were steeper than 1 in 50. However, here on the route of the old Torrington & Marland Railway, curves could be as sharp as 9 chains and gradients as steep as 1 in 42, although the original narrow-gauge line was even steeper, at 1 in 30.

Right: There are a couple of passengers on the platform as we enter Dunsbear Halt on an up Torrington-bound train in 1961. Dunsbear had no loop and only one platform; the simple buildings incorporated a waiting room, goods store and office. 23 chains south from here was the connection to the Marland North Devon Clay Company, which until 1970 operated an extensive 3-foot-gauge system in the clay workings. Between here and Torrington the line largely followed the route of the Torrington & Marland Light Railway, except for a short deviation beyond Yarde to avoid the steep gradients of the narrow-gauge summit.

Right: The driver of No 41314 strikes a pose at the north end of Petrockstow station on 23 May 1961, while awaiting departure for Torrington at 11.26am. The first of these Ivatt 2-6-2 tanks arrived in the West of England during 1952; following a successful trial by one on the branch in March 1953, they replaced the previous 'E1/R' 0-6-2Ts later that year. Being a light railway, the ND&CJLR was well endowed with level crossings: nine on public roads, 81 occupation crossings, four footpaths and one bridleway. As seen here, the roads were protected by cattle guards.

Left: This is the southern end of the up platform at Petrockstow on the occasion of the 'Exmoor Ranger' tour; the station platforms here were the longest on the ND&CJLR at 200ft, the others being 167ft. It was the busiest of the three main intermediate stations passenger-wise, although the total for Petrockstow, Hatherleigh and Hole was only about 2,300 in 1936; the 1920 estimate before construction had been 70,000. Petrockstow ground frame is visible in the foreground, and to the left is one of the two sidings provided in the goods yard, where there was an animal feedstuffs store. Other traffic here was coal, milk (between 1929 and 1936), general merchandise and livestock (204 trucks of which were despatched in 1930).

WHISTLE

The isolated ball clay deposits around Meeth had to wait for exploitation until the opening of the ND&CJLR in 1925. China clay remains in the place it was formed, whereas ball clay is sedimentary, ie carried by streams and deposited in low-lying areas. By the mid-1970s underground working had been abandoned and production was from pits; this photograph was taken during the visit of the 'Devon Rambler' railtour on 20 April 1974. The railway onwards to Halwill closed in 1965. Note the incorrect spellings on the ticket.

On Saturday 15 June 1963 the afternoon single-coach train from Torrington to Halwill behind No 41313 is taking water at Hatherleigh. This was the most important intermediate station on the line, the Stationmaster here also being responsible for Hole, Meeth and Petrockstow. The first sod of the ND&CJLR was ceremoniously cut near here at Lewer Bridge on 30 June 1922 by Arthur Neal MP, Parliamentary Secretary to the Minister of Transport. The last day for passenger traffic was Saturday 27 February 1965, freight continuing until the autumn of that year along the short section to Hatherleigh from the Meeth clay sidings.

Right: This scene of rural tranquillity at Hatherleigh, with the morning Halwill–Torrington service taking water in 1961, contrasts with the 'Hatherleigh Riots' of 23 June 1923. Twenty unemployed men had been sent from Plymouth to help the existing navvies in building the ND&CJLR; however, these newcomers did not want the type of manual labour involved. After some hours of drinking things got a little rowdy and Sergeant Babb suggested they return to camp; a scuffle ensued and he was knocked to the ground several times. PC Hutchings stood over him and saved his life, fighting off the crowd amidst a hail of bottles, sticks and stones. The hooligans received sentences of hard labour.

Right: Hole for Black Torrington was the final station on the ND&CJLR before Halwill, and the morning service from Halwill to Torrington is exchanging tablets there on 23 May 1961; the line was worked by Tyers No 6 electric tablet equipment. A surprising traffic flow through Hole, before closure to freight in September 1964, was North Devon clay, being worked to Halwill for onwards travel along the North Cornwall line, eventually to Lostwithiel and Fowey Docks. This complicated routeing involved reversals at Halwill, Wadebridge, Bodmin General and Bodmin Road. When combined with the Wenford clay at Boscarne Junction, two 'Ns' were needed to get it up the bank to Bodmin General.

This view of Hole for Black Torrington looking towards Hatherleigh was taken during Whitsun 1965 after closure of the line; passenger services had ceased in the February and freight the previous September. The points and signals were operated by the small open ground frame visible on the left, tablet instruments being housed in the station building. The passing loop could hold 22 wagons. The second picture is an 8mm ciné film frame taken in the summer of 1963, and shows plenty of traffic in Hole's two sidings.

Weeds have already started to grow on the track at Hole, less than three months after the last special train passed through — the 'Exmoor Ranger' — on 27 March 1965. Hole was a winding 3 miles and 7 chains from Halwill, crossing desolate Devon countryside and involving gradients as steep as 1 in 50. The station buildings of rough stone masonry are on the up (Torrington) platform with the two goods sidings behind. It was originally proposed to call this station Black Torrington, but instead it was named after a hamlet/farm some miles away, probably to avoid confusion with Torrington itself.

HOLE
FOR BLACK TORRINGTON

We have now arrived at Halwill. When the first line through here to Holsworthy from Meldon Junction, Okehampton, opened in January 1879 the station was called Beaworthy, but this was changed in July 1879 to Halwill & Beaworthy. It was changed to Halwill Junction in 1887 after opening of the Launceston line, and finally to Halwill for Beaworthy in 1923. However, it still continued to be referred to as Halwill Junction after 1923, and even today, decades after complete closure, the village is called Halwill Junction. The notices on the hoarding in the background of this Whitsun 1966 shot include one for a wrestling competition at Exeter Civic Hall on 12 May featuring Tony St

Right: At Halwill the splitting of the Bude section from the rear of the Padstow-bound down 'Atlantic Coast Express' was fairly straightforward. One or two coaches would be detached and the Bude branch engine, already with its two-coach 'P' set, would back on, then head for Bude, all done in about 5 minutes. It was a different matter with the up 'ACE', seen arriving at Halwill on 23 May 1961 behind 'Battle of Britain' No 34072 *257 Squadron.* The Bude section will have arrived at the same platform a few minutes earlier, the locomotive then running round and taking the coaches back out in the Bude direction. After the Padstow section arrives the Bude coach(es) will be attached at the rear, No 34072 then taking the combined train on to Okehampton; this took about 10 minutes.

Left: The attachments made, the up 'Atlantic Coast Express' is now ready to leave for Okehampton. Note that unrebuilt *257 Squadron* (the rebuilt engines were too heavy for this route) still has the upward extension of the tender sides at the rear, called raves. In September 1943 a large freight yard with capacity for about 250 wagons was opened here for US Army ammunition supplies, on the up side (towards Okehampton). The signal on the left of the bracket is for trains entering the associated reception loop, which had a 60-wagon capacity.

'N' class No 31838 is by Halwill signalbox during August 1961 with a freight, including two brake-vans. The goods trains off both the Bude and North Cornwall lines arrived here at similar times in the afternoon, shunting taking place between them (the other goods appears to be shrouded in steam in the distance).

The signalbox had four separate tablet machines for the single lines to Ashbury, Ashwater, Dunsland Cross and Hole. An extension was added to it when the Torrington line opened, and it was reputed to be the largest signalbox on any single-line system in the country.

The date on the back of the ticket is 15 June 1963, and it was purchased to travel on this train, the 6.22pm for Launceston and the North Cornwall line, seen arriving at Halwill from Okehampton behind 'N'-class Mogul No 31845. This efficient and successful class arrived in the area in 1924; there were still 21 on Exmouth Junction's books at the beginning of 1964, the last full year of steam. Considerably more powerful than the 'Jubilee'-class 0-4-2s and the various 4-4-0s, as well as being able to use the existing 50ft turntables, the 'Ns' became the workhorses of both passenger and freight services in the West.

In this 27 March 1965 view of the 'Exmoor Ranger' tour at Halwill, the goods yard is empty following withdrawal of freight facilities during September 1964. Most of the wagon sorting from the various converging routes took place on the running lines, the goods yard being mainly for local traffic. Partly visible on the extreme right is the brick-built slaughterhouse, which had generated considerable traffic, latterly in demountable containers attached to eastbound afternoon passenger trains (mainly for London's Smithfield Market). Eggs were perhaps the most surprising traffic, 100,000 being despatched daily! There was also a turntable in the yard, not visible from here, on the distant right forking track.

Some of the 200-plus enthusiasts from the 'Exmoor Ranger' tour are wandering about the tracks. Just visible above the cab of the closest Ivatt Class 2 can be seen the top of a large water tank, which, in addition to supplying locomotives, also fed the cattle wagon washing points. Both the down main and bay starting signal pairs date from 1934, when the height of the signals was altered. It was possible for simultaneous departures of North Cornwall and Bude services, although this was not common practice.

This panoramic view of Halwill was taken at Whitsun 1965. There is a single-unit railcar in the bay on the left; DMUs took over after the demise of steam on the Bude and North Cornwall lines at the beginning of January 1965. The track is still *in situ* on the closed North Devon & Cornwall Junction line on the right. The very last steam working here was for the centenary of the GWR line to Launceston, on 5 September 1965, using No 41283.

HALWILL FOR BEAWORTHY
JUNCTION FOR BUDE NORTH CORNWALL & TORRINGTON LINES

TICKET OFFICE

Standard Class 4 2-6-4 tank No 80040 has just arrived at Halwill from Bude on Saturday 15 June 1963. When the former Southern Region areas of Devon and Cornwall were transferred to Western Region control on 1 January 1963 there were 12 of this class, including No 80040, allocated to Exmouth Junction shed (83D). Of these, two were sub-shedded at Exmouth and one each at Bude, Launceston and Okehampton. Eastleigh Works ceased giving general repairs to the class in April 1964, and those stopped for repairs thereafter were condemned; unlucky No 80040 was withdrawn on 6 May 1964, despatched to Crewe and cut up in July.

There are plenty of signal cables and point rodding in the foreground, kept safely out of the way under a wooden walkway in the middle distance. No 41314 is in the Torrington bay, having arrived with the morning train on 23 May 1961. Immediately to the left can just be seen the Bude portion of the up 'Atlantic Coast Express', awaiting attachment to the rear of the yet-to-arrive Padstow portion. In the distance is a signal post with arms facing in opposite directions, and to the left are five demountable containers for the local slaughterhouse traffic. The building on the left is a pump house.

The now preserved Ivatt Class 2 No 41313 has arrived at Halwill on the afternoon service from Torrington on Saturday 15 June 1963. It is still displaying the Southern Region shed code for Barnstaple Junction (72E), although since this area had been transferred to Western Region control at the beginning of the year technically it should have been an 83F plate. The Torrington line signalling was largely self-contained at Halwill and worked by ground frames, like the one by the signal that is allowing No 41313 to reverse back past the long 'N'-hauled freight on the Bude branch, to its own separate run-round loop.

This view from a Bude-bound railcar leaving Halwill during the spring of 1966 shows two 'D63xx' diesel-hydraulics 'topping and tailing' an engineering train on the North Cornwall line. The wooden building to the side of the diesel is a permanent-way trolley shed. A lattice arrangement with strong guying has been used in the construction of the signal post that carries both the down starter (LSWR lower-quadrant) and up home (SR upper-quadrant) for the Launceston line. In comparison, the up home from the Bude branch is a substantial steel structure. Note the new 109lb/yd flat-bottom rail on pre-stressed concrete sleepers; four months later all services had been withdrawn.

Right: Immediately after the junction at Halwill, the North Cornwall line took this sharp 20-chain-radius curve on its way to join the valley of the River Carey, which it followed most of the way down to Launceston. No D6330 is at the rear of the engineering train seen in the previous picture, waiting to gain entry to Halwill. The line was opened to Launceston in July 1886, and there were passing loops at both intermediate stations of Ashwater and Tower Hill. By 1966 'rationalisation' had seen both loops taken out of use (November 1965), creating a 12½-mile single-line section.

Right: 'T9' No 30715 is making its way through the large tree plantations near Dunsland Cross in April 1960. Judging by the disc code displayed on the smokebox, it is the afternoon through service from Bude to Okehampton. Note the large eight-wheeled 'water cart' tender, very useful for the long non-stop runs without water troughs that the class used to undertake in their heyday. The 'T9s' at this time were the oldest express passenger engines still at work in the country but in just over a year's time all would be withdrawn. One member survives in preservation. *M. J. Esau*

Dunsland Cross was an isolated station and the least busy on the Bude branch, issuing just 4,478 tickets in 1928. It broke up the section from Halwill to Holsworthy, although not many services were booked to pass here. This Whitsun 1965 view is looking towards Halwill. Attached to the station sign is 'ALIGHT HERE FOR SHEBBEAR COLLEGE' (a boys' college), although this was miles away. In the general run-down of services before final closure the signalbox was closed on 2 January 1966, the down loop being retained for the remaining passenger-only service until the end came in October of that year.

The construction contract for the branch from Meldon Junction to a terminus at Holsworthy started in August 1875, and opening day here at Holsworthy was 20 January 1879. Work commenced on the extension to Bude at the end of 1896, and it opened on Wednesday 10 August 1898 with a directors' special. The original single platform of 1879 (made of local stone) is on the left, and when the extension was opened a platform (of brick) was built alongside the existing run-round loop on the right. In this 1965 view, looking east, note the original canopy of 1879 and the Stationmaster's house complete with large greenhouse.

This 10 June 1965 shot (the same date as the ticket) at Whitstone & Bridgerule is looking east. This was the only intermediate station on the extension from Holsworthy to Bude, and still has the original LSWR-style nameboard. The station was built on a 30-chain-radius curve, and the loop accommodated 35 wagons.

For much of its length the River Tamar marks the border between Devon and Cornwall, but here, since 1832 and despite being west of the Tamar, we are in a small area of Devon jutting into Cornwall. Closure to freight came in September 1964 and passenger services finished in October 1966.

This is the view looking towards Bude on the same day, when the child's ticket to Holsworthy was issued (note the change of price). At the west end of the station was a 45-foot-deep sheer-sided cutting through shale and rock, crossed by an overbridge formed of concrete blocks. In 1943 the US Army needed a yard here for ammunition trains, and about 150ft of the down platform was removed to allow entry into two newly built sidings about a quarter of a mile long. The sidings were taken up in 1947 and the platform restored, hence the different construction styles on either side of the signalbox.

The LSWR provided Bude with quite extensive station buildings commensurate with the expected summer traffic. The photograph was most likely taken on the same date that the platform ticket was purchased — Thursday 2 June 1966. The station was built in red brick with quoins and decorations in Portland stone, and included (from left to right) a porters' room, a large gents' toilet, a ladies' waiting room, a general waiting room, a booking hall and office, a refreshment room (shut by this time) and a substantial two-storey house for the Stationmaster. Deep piling was required for the foundations, as it was built on boggy ground. All would be demolished after closure later in the year.

The afternoon passenger service from here at Bude ran separately from the North Cornwall line trains after the early 1930s, and was regularly hauled by a 4-4-0 from Okehampton, arriving around 2.15pm and leaving about an hour later. The date is Wednesday 24 May 1961, and 'T9' No 30709 is displaying the Exeter–Padstow headcode. This service also carried perishable traffic, in vans and wagons at the rear, to give a faster transit than the daily freights. The siding on the left was added as part of the 1939 alterations to increase capacity; previously it was an attractive garden with acacia palms.

The colour (Ektachrome) view shows No 30709 leaving Bude on the afternoon through service to Okehampton on the same day, 24 May 1961. It was taken by the author's late father, his location being the coaling stage midway between the engine shed and water tank. That's the author (aged nine) in short trousers on the station platform, having just taken the inset black & white photograph. On the extreme right is the goods shed, and behind the wagons is a store built in the 1930s for fertiliser traffic. The cattle pens between the cattle wagon and No 30709 were busy when animals were driven down on the hoof from Stratton Market.

It is 9.30am on the same morning, and Standard Class 3 tank No 82011 is leaving Bude for Halwill. Prominent in the background is Bude Gasworks. The Bude Gas Company started production in about 1900, some of the coal coming by sea, and the works visible here date from enlargement in the 1950s; it used about six wagons of coal a day. At first sight the circular dot below the locomotive number might be taken for the WR yellow route availability code; in fact it is the yellow spot used by the SR to indicate that No 82011 was equipped with the French TIA (Traitement Integral Armand) water-softening system.

Left: 'N'-class Mogul No 31857, allocated to 72A (Exmouth Junction), shunts at Bude during May 1961; to the right is the open coal stage by the side of the road to the shed and turntable, and beyond the gasworks can again be seen. No 31857 is coupled to two meat container wagons for the local slaughterhouse trade. This important traffic was sent overnight to Nine Elms (in southwest London) for Smithfield Market, or to Birmingham, in which case the routeing was via the Somerset & Dorset line from Templecombe to Bath. The facility to transfer these containers to road transport in the cities allowed greater flexibility.

Left: The first 'N'-class 2-6-0 arrived at Exmouth Junction for trials in 1924. They revolutionised freight working in the far west and were still operating to Bude when goods services were withdrawn in September 1964. Over all those years one would leave Exmouth Junction at about 3.30am on the Bude goods, and after 2-3 hours shunting here at Bude (including down to the canal basin and servicing at the shed) it would head back. It was important to be at Halwill for around 4.45pm to connect with the North Cornwall line goods. No 31857 will not get back to Exeter until around 9pm — a long day's work.

The main platform face at Bude was 570ft long. No 82023 is on the loop and will eventually couple up to the two-coach 'P' set positioned by the station canopy. Seen during August 1961, the locomotive is displaying the single-disc headcode for a Bude–Halwill working. The shed code is 72A (Exmouth Junction), to which No 82023 had been allocated following construction at Swindon in October 1954. 'SC' below the shed code indicates a self-cleaning smokebox. These British Railways-designed Standard Class 3 tank engines achieved some high mileages between Heavy General overhauls; No 82023 attained 196,756 miles and had its first boiler change in 1959.

Left: In this June 1965 view at Bude, to the right of the standard LSWR signalbox is a milepost indicating 228 miles from London Waterloo. Behind the milepost is the concrete fence erected in the 1920s to stop locomotive ash blowing about, and also the 49ft 10in turntable (although Bude shed had closed the previous September). To the left is a permanent way trolley hut. In preparation for the June 1939 Royal Cornwall Show at Bude, considerable alterations were made, including moving the starting signals on the right 114ft towards the signalbox; this permitted a divided 15-coach train to be loaded simultaneously in the main and bay platforms.

Left: Bude shed was a sub of Exmouth Junction all its life and opened with the line. From the early days its allocation was one 0-4-4T (two in summer). The water tank had already lost its roof before this June 1966 shot. The run-round loop looks to have had very little use recently as there was no freight traffic by this time and the passenger service was in the hands of diesel railcars. In the last years of steam the allocation was generally BR Standard tanks, initially from the '82xxx' series (from 1952), then the '80xxx' (from 1962). The shed closed in September 1964, although steam working continued to Bude until the beginning of January 1965.

Right: Pressure of work created by the extra summer services to Bude required more temporary staff. Before World War 2 lodgings were found in the town, but subsequently old coaches were used as dormitories. The author's research reveals that initially an old LSWR sleeping car was used, followed by a converted Maunsell coach. This photograph, taken on 24 May 1961 by the headshunt beyond Bude station (adjacent to the siding added in 1939), features an ex-LNWR 12-wheel sleeping car which, according to the note on the back of the print, had been built at Wolverton *c*1905; now numbered DM198929, it would be gone by August.

Right: Bude's namesake, 'West Country' Pacific No 34006, is seen, still with its extra-long smoke-deflector wings, in Yeovil shed yard, close by Yeovil Town station, on 27 March 1963, When newly built *Bude* (then numbered 21C106) was named by the Chairman of Bude Urban District Council on 1 November 1945. The class did not regularly work to Bude, as the turntable was not long enough to turn them. However, No 34006 was more widely travelled than most, having participated in the 1948 Locomotive Exchanges, its performance being described by C. J. Allen as 'sheer brilliance'; on 11 June that year, between Leicester and Rugby, it achieved 2,010hp — the highest equivalent drawbar horsepower of any locomotive tested.

Left: An Act of Parliament for the Bude Canal was obtained in 1819, and it was in operation by 1823, eventually totalling 35½ miles in length. It was unique in that it was built for agricultural purposes, transporting lime-rich sand from Bude beach for use as fertiliser. The coming of the railway sealed its fate; part was abandoned in the 1890s, and in 1902 it was sold to the local council, which used the upper reaches to provide a potable water supply. This is the scene at Helebridge, about 1½ miles from Bude, on 22 May 1961, showing the abandoned canal through the arch of the railway bridge and looking towards the Camelford road bridge. During construction of the railway, the canal was used to transport materials that had arrived by sea at Bude.

Left: To gain height, the canal used six inclined planes, including this one at Marhamchurch, also photographed on 22 May 1961. The canal barges, called tub boats, were equipped with wheels to allow for passage onto the rails of the inclined planes. A continuous chain was used to tow the tub boats up and down, driven by underground water wheels set in wheel pits at the head of each plane. Following the arrival of the railway at Holsworthy in 1879 the canal went into decline and abandonment.

Standard Class 4 tank No 80067 is waiting for custom at Bude on 11 August 1963 before departing at 6.45pm. This locomotive worked in the far south-west from May 1962 until September 1964 when it was transferred to Templecombe for Somerset and Dorset services, withdrawal coming in June 1965 from Bristol (Barrow Road) depot. After the closure of Bude shed in September 1964 steam carried on until the beginning of January 1965 using the facilities at Okehampton. Interestingly in this final steam period Standard Class 4 tender engines of the 75xxx series were used and, as they were too long to be turned on Bude's turntable, this involved tender-first operation. *P. Paye*

The sea lock of the Bude Canal is visible on the left, while on the right the course of the River Neet was altered to create a deep channel for vessels manoeuvring on the tides. Sand was dug up from the Summerleaze beach here and transported to the canal by a horse-drawn railway. For 100 years from 1823 a 4ft 0in plateway was used; then, in late 1923, a 2ft 0in tramway was acquired and laid on the formation of the plateway. The tramway is seen in this 1965 view descending the 1 in 50 incline to the beach; it was last used in 1942.

This page: The nearest Austin A40 (DFJ 287C, registered in Exeter) would have been about a year old in June 1966, when this view was recorded of the Lower Basin of the Bude Canal. There was little direct sea/rail commercial intercourse; however, the 360ft of siding along Bude UDC's private wharf here was extended westward in 1907 by 150ft to allow sea sand from the plateway to be tipped into railway wagons. Much valued by local farmers, the sand was also shipped to water works (for filter beds) and golf links. At its maximum the siding could hold 30 wagons; however, the length was reduced in both 1940 and 1955 before closure in 1964.

We are now taking the North Cornwall line from Halwill, and have arrived at Launceston, where, on a pleasant summer's evening, an 'N'-class Mogul is having its 4,000-gallon tender topped up. The date is Saturday 15 June 1963 and the road ahead is clear for the all-stations 7.26pm departure to Halwill and Okehampton. The left-hand signal is for the wartime spur connecting the adjacent (but until then separate) Great Western and Southern systems at Launceston. It was opened on 22 September 1943 for munitions traffic but not inter-company transfers until it came into regular use from 30 June 1952 when the Western Region passenger service from Plymouth was transferred to this station.

Right: The 'Atlantic Coast Express' is leaving Launceston for London behind No 34078 *222 Squadron* on Thursday 12 June 1962. Nearest to us is GWR light Prairie tank No 4567, which will, once the Bulleid Pacific is clear, move to the up platform and form the mid-morning service to Plymouth via Tavistock South. The Plymouth line closed to passengers at the end of December 1962 in blizzard conditions, and freight from Launceston to Lifton finished at the same time. However, when the North Cornwall line freight services ceased in September 1964, the GWR route was re-opened from the Ambrosia Dairy at Lifton to provide a goods service for Launceston until February 1966.

Right: Launceston is still doing a good business in parcels with this Wadebridge-bound railcar during Whitsun 1966, despite complete closure being only a few months away. The LSWR signalbox, on the up platform, had been enlarged in 1917 to accommodate a GWR frame and token instrument for the adjacent GWR station. The passing loops at Launceston, Egloskerry and Tresmeer were surprisingly short and problems could result, although the only really long passenger train in later years was the Summer Saturday 11.0am Padstow–Waterloo, still 10 coaches in 1961 but only seven in 1963. The footbridge from which this view was taken drew early criticism for being too steep.

Left: The Launceston Agricultural Society's Show of July 1892 coincided with the opening of the line west to Tresmeer. The only intermediate station beyond Launceston, here at Egloskerry, had not been finished, so it opened later in October. Egloskerry's passing loop could only hold a locomotive and seven passenger coaches or 23 freight wagons (including brake van), so careful regulating of long trains was needed; its main buildings are in standard North Cornwall Railway style. A level crossing at the Tresmeer end (behind us) ensured that the signalbox stayed open until closure of the line in October 1966, although freight facilities had been withdrawn in 1961.

Left: The fact that no signals are visible gives a clue as to the date of this summer afternoon picture of Tresmeer station. Freight had ceased in September 1964, the signalbox closed on 14 November 1965, and the line closed in October 1966, so it is the summer of 1966 — actually early June. There were by now three trains each way, and they used the down (far) platform, where the lamp posts have had their lamps removed. In the background is the corrugated iron lamp room, beyond which is the brick-built goods shed (still with weed-covered rails) and behind again are six staff cottages built by the LSWR.

Right: This is Camelford in the summer of 1962, with 'N'-class 2-6-0 No 31841 ready to leave for Wadebridge, taken on Perutz film. The town of Camelford was not well regarded; the 1769 turnpike road avoided it, and it was disenfranchised in the 1832 Reform Act. The station was 1½ miles from the town, for at the time of its construction the engineers were more concerned with providing access to Delabole Quarry. However, it was an important railhead for the area (including Tintagel and Boscastle) and, indicative of its status, had an awning over the up platform. At 700ft above sea level it could be very wet and windy, so slate cladding was used for the Stationmaster's house.

Right: The date is Friday 8 July 1960 and the location Dunmere Junction. No 30587 is heading up the valley of the River Camel with its usual load of empties for the china-clay works near Wenford Bridge. The line in the foreground is the branch to Bodmin North; in 1964 it was this short section of line between Boscarne Junction and Bodmin North that saw the introduction of a railbus service connecting with trains from Bodmin General, instead of through services to Wadebridge. The goods workings were also revised with a Drewry diesel-shunter making trips as required to Bodmin North in addition to the Wenford branch; the steeply-graded Bodmin North branch closed in 1967.
J. C. Haydon

Left: On 25 May 1961 No 30586 shunts at Wadebridge in the down sidings to the south of the station, with the goods shed on the right and cattle pens on the left — most survived until final closure at Wadebridge in 1978. These Beattie well tanks also took a hand in local passenger workings right up to withdrawal, latterly to cover for unreliability of the WR 'D63xx' diesel-hydraulics. On 7 December 1961, following a derailment and a collision, Nos 30585/6 were used all day on the Padstow and Bodmin North services. Alone among the three survivors of the class, No 30586 was cut up upon withdrawal; happily, the other two live on in preservation.

Below: Of the three long-surviving Beattie tanks at Wadebridge, No 30586 was a little different. Nos 30585/7 were both built by Beyer Peacock in 1873, whereas No 30586 emerged two years later, and had square splashers to the driving wheels. It also apparently had a higher tank filler cap, which meant that it was more difficult to fill up at the water stop in Pencarrow Woods on the way up to Wenford Bridge. So, given a choice the crews would leave No 30586 at Wadebridge, as here on 25 May 1961. In addition to station pilot duties it was used on the sharply curved sidings at Wadebridge Quay.

Right: During the 69-year association of the Beattie tanks with the Wenford Bridge branch replacements were considered. In September 1900 an Adams 'O2' 0-4-4 tank was sent for trial, and an 'Ilfracombe Goods' was next, but neither were suitable. In 1928 a Wainwright 'P' class had a go, as did 0-6-0 tank *A. S. Harris* from the Callington branch, but again neither was suitable. It was not until 1962, when this photo was taken adjacent to Wadebridge shed, that suitable replacements were found in the form of Great Western-built dock tanks of the '1366' class, their combination of short wheelbase and light axle load proving a success.

Left: No 30585 has just arrived at the Wenford china-clay works with a string of empties on a sunny 22 September 1959. After the Cornwall and Devon Central Railway failed in 1846 there was much pressure in Cornwall for a standard-gauge line to compete against the broad-gauge camp. This already existing line from Wenford Bridge down the valley of the River Camel was used in an 1864 Act of Parliament authorising construction of the Launceston, Bodmin and Wadebridge Junction Railway. This involved a new line from Launceston to Wenford Bridge with running powers thence over the Bodmin and Wadebridge. However, the company suffered the fate of so many of the period and was unable to raise the finance.

Left: Class N Mogul No 31855 arrives at Wadebridge from Padstow during June 1962. The introduction of new main-line coaching stock from 1946 allowed the prewar equivalents to be cascaded to secondary work, and in 1949 two-coach 'P' sets 22-29 were formed from this older stock. The first coach in 'P' set 24 seen here is a Maunsell flush-panelled Brake Third. We are standing on the original 1888 platform; the 350ft island platform opposite dates from 1899 and was originally supported by timber and iron struts to a newer standard platform height of 3ft. It suffered from sagging and was gradually replaced by a mix of pre-cast concrete (as here) and concrete blocks.

Below: This is the east end of Wadebridge station and yards in October 1979. The North Cornwall line closed from 3 October 1966, the Bodmin Road–Padstow passenger service following from 30 January 1967; the two signalboxes here (East and West) closed in December of that year, after which the line to Wadebridge from Boscarne Junction was treated as a long siding. Molesworth Street crossing gates were closed for good after the quay sidings closed in April 1973. Latterly fertiliser in sacks from Avonmouth was the main traffic, but even this ceased from 4 September 1978.

To cross wide Little Petherick Creek between Padstow and Wadebridge, a combination of a 200-yard embankment faced with concrete blocks and a 400ft viaduct were used, all on a curve of 20-chain radius. Originally an opening bridge was proposed, but by 1896 larger vessels no longer used Tregaske's Quay in the creek. In February 1898 ironwork was delivered by barge from Wadebridge to build the wrought iron girder spans resting on four 8ft-diameter cast-iron cylinders, driven through 53ft of mud to reach rock. Our Wadebridge-bound train is being hauled by 'T9' No 30717 on Thursday 25 May 1961. Today the bridge forms part of the 'Camel Trail' cycle route.

In their twilight years the 'T9' 4-4-0s were associated with the 'Withered Arm', as here with No 30717 about to leave Padstow on 25 May 1961, the date of this child's ticket. When built between 1899 and 1901 the 'T9s' were the LSWR's premier express locomotives and earned the nickname 'Greyhounds' because of their free running and speed. All 66 were superheated in the 1920s, and this is when they first appeared at Padstow. Exmouth Junction had 10 in 1932, and soon afterwards Wadebridge received an allocation. During World War 2 they could be seen double-heading long troop trains, but by the time of this photograph they were down to single figures, and all would be gone by July.

Left: Boscarne Junction came about in 1888 on the opening of the line from Bodmin GWR that connected with the already existing line from Bodmin LSWR. Here on 22 September 1959 Beattie well tank 30585 passes the signal box whilst shunting traffic between the two systems. *P. Q. Treloar*

Below: This colourful shot of pannier tank No 4666 leaving Bodmin North for Wadebridge was taken during June 1962. The Bodmin & Wadebridge Railway had been constructed quite early on, opening in 1834, its main purpose being not passenger traffic but to convey limey sea sand from Wadebridge up the valley of the River Camel, where it was much in demand as fertiliser. The company was, however, fond of running passenger excursions; on 13 April 1840 one was run from Wadebridge to see two public executions at Bodmin Gaol, and it proved so popular that three trains were run, carrying 1,100 passengers.

Right: Sharp curves abounded on the Wenford Bridge branch and for much of the distance there was no fencing; drivers had to be prepared to stop short of any obstruction. All movements had to be made in daylight, and a 20-ton brake-van (at least) had to be attached at the rear. In later years the china-clay traffic was an important source of revenue, and curving away behind the first two wagons are returning china-clay empties. In this 25 May 1961 view No 30587, a Beattie '0298'-class 2-4-0WT (the oldest design then still in use on BR) is approaching the china-clay works.

Left: No 30586 is again on its usual station pilot duties at Wadebridge on 15 August 1959, having just added some vans to the coaches in the 1888 platform. This platform was extended in 1899 to a total of 460 feet by extensions at both ends on completion of the line to Padstow. Originally there was an ornate wooden footbridge connecting with the 1899 island platform this view is taken from; however; it was replaced by the basic concrete structure visible here in the 1920s. Note the cantilevered awning provided on the station offices, adjacent to the coaches; prior to 1915 the booking office in here had separate LSWR and GWR positions. *D. Fereday-Glenn*

Left: Sister well tank No 30585 is crossing the Bodmin–Wadebridge main road with the daily train to Wenford Bridge in August 1961. Timings did not vary that much over the years; in 1909 the departure from Wadebridge was 9.58am and the return departure from the clay sidings 2.0pm; in 1962 the times were 9.35am from Wadebridge and 1.55pm from the clay sidings. The 1962 replacements for these Victorian veterans, the GWR dock tanks, lasted only two years, and the last two steam trips up the branch, for enthusiasts, ran on 19 September and 31 October 1964.

Left: This lovely shot shows No 30587 again on the lower reaches of the Wenford Bridge branch during June 1962, just before the GWR tanks from Weymouth Docks took over. While the three Beattie tanks were associated with this service for 69 years their replacements only worked it for two years, before being displaced by Drewry diesel shunters. The estimate for the construction of this section of line from the turnpike road near Dunmeer (sic) to Tresarrett Bridge in 1831 was £6,371 12s 4d, and that for the whole of the Bodmin & Wadebridge Railway was £21,882 9s 4d (not including engines, rolling-stock and

Right: The Bodmin & Wadebridge Railway chose the standard gauge (4ft 8½in) for its line, which was unusual at the time; the clay lines to the south were 4ft 0in-gauge. To generate traffic the company built a number of wharves along the route, and this is Dunmere Siding (formerly Borough Bounds Wharf), close by the crossing of the Wadebridge–Bodmin main road, in June 1962. The original Perutz slide is badly damaged, but thanks to computer-based photographic programmes it is now possible to repair and enhance damaged slides (but not fake) and achieve the result seen here.

Above: Wenford china-clay works, about half a mile short of the terminus, generated most of the traffic on the line at this time. The high-quality clay was pumped 6 miles to here from mines on Stannon Moor; it was then dried and processed before being loaded into the railway wagons. The Bodmin & Wadebridge Railway regarded the Wenford route as its main line, and in the mid-1840s it considered going further up the Camel Valley with an extension to the great slate quarry at Delabole. No 30587 is pictured, again on 25 May 1961. The line closed in 1983.

Right: Our final view of No 30587 shows it shunting at the china-clay works on the same day. There were no regular passenger services up the branch, but excursions were run from the very beginning. On 14 June 1837 an excursion left Wadebridge at 11.0am for Wenford Bridge with about 400 passengers in 27 vehicles, double-headed by the entire locomotive stock of the Bodmin & Wadebridge Railway, *Camel* and *Elephant*. Receipts totalled £26 11s 6d.

Half a mile beyond the china clay works was the terminus of the line at the goods depot of Wenford Bridge; it had opened in 1834 and was 11 miles and 63 chains from Wadebridge. When connected to the rest of the LSWR system in 1895 this was the furthest point from Waterloo, although it never had a regular passenger service. The layout here was altered in 1926 to give a long run-round loop and two additional sidings, one of which connected with the De Lank Quarries via a cable incline. This photograph of No 30585 was taken on 22 September 1959, the goods depot closing in 1967. *P. Q. Treloar*